BOOKWORMS

Animal Homes

A Fox's Den

Arthur Best

Cavendish Square
New York

Published in 2019 by Cavendish Square Publishing, LLC
243 5th Avenue, Suite 136, New York, NY 10016

First Edition

Website: cavendishsq.com

Library of Congress Cataloging-in-Publication Data

Names: Best, B. J., 1976- author.
Title: A fox's den / Arthur Best.
Description: First edition. | New York : Cavendish Square, 2019. |
Series: Animal homes | Audience: Grades K-2. | Includes index.
Identifiers: LCCN 2017048037 (print) | LCCN 2017054688 (ebook) | ISBN 9781502636546 (library bound) |
ISBN 9781502636560 (pbk.) | ISBN 9781502636577 (6 pack) | ISBN 9781502636553 (ebook)
Subjects: LCSH: Foxes--Habitations--Juvenile literature. | Foxes--Juvenile literature.
Classification: LCC QL737.C22 (ebook) | LCC QL737.C22 B477 2019 (print) | DDC 599.775--dc23
LC record available at https://lccn.loc.gov/2017048037

Editorial Director: David McNamara
Copy Editor: Rebecca Rohan
Associate Art Director: Amy Greenan
Designer: Megan Mette
Production Coordinator: Karol Szymczuk
Photo Research: J8 Media

The photographs in this book are used by permission and through the courtesy of: Cover Geoffrey Kuchera/Shutterstock.com; p. 5 Menno Schaefer/Shutterstock.com; p. 7 Jamie Hall/Shutterstock.com; p. 9 Don Johnston/WU/Alamy Sttock Photo; p. 11, 13 Juniors Bildarchiv GmbH/Alamy Stock Photo; p. 15 Menno Schaefer/Shutterstock.com; p. 17 Les Stocker/Oxford Scientific/Getty Images; p. 19 Michael Francis Photography/Animals Animals; p. 21 Richard Seeley Photography/Moment/Getty Images.

Printed in the United States of America

Contents

A fox is the size of a dog.

Foxes live near trees.

They live near fields.

A fox hunts at night.

It eats mice.

It eats rabbits.

It also eats berries.

It rests in the day.

A fox rests in its **den**.

The den is the fox's home!

The den is **underground**.

The fox can dig.

It digs a room.

Other animals also dig holes.

A fox can use their holes.

It is cold in winter.

Foxes must hunt for food.

Then they go home.

Dens keep foxes **warm**.

Foxes have babies in winter.

The babies live in the den.

They are called **cubs**.

The den is safe.

Cubs grow there.

Cubs grow up.

They will dig a new den!

New Words

cubs (CUBS) Baby foxes.

dens (DENZ) Homes of foxes.

underground (UN-der-GROUND) Below Earth's surface.

warm (WARM) Not quite hot.

Index

About the Author

Arthur Best lives in Wisconsin with his wife and son. He has written many other books for children. He has seen a red fox in his driveway.

About BOOKWORMS

Bookworms help independent readers gain reading confidence through high-frequency words, simple sentences, and strong picture/text support. Each book explores a concept that helps children relate what they read to the world they live in.